Managers Must Perform

the non-academic advice from a winner on how to be a star manager

Dr. Paul Ola Kazeem,
Productivity Merit Award, and Championship
Award Winner

*Practical thoughts for practical minds.
What the professionals left out, and
Managers weren't taught in colleges
about their positions.*

Dedication

To my mum Ajoke Kazeem who told me at 10 years old that I will be great; my Dad, S.B. Kazeem, the most kind hearted man that ever lived, a successful business mogul of Ikereku Land, who taught me to believe that everyone can be a success

And

To all heroes and heroines, ordinary folks who made extra ordinary strides and left us footprints to challenge us to higher pursuits

Table of Contents

Legacy

Dr. Paul Kazeem is an avid writer, business consultant, and a motivational speaker, who had made tremendous impact on thousands of people. He had authored other books such as The Making of a Star; Make Yourself Important; and several poetry works including 'She Prints on the Rocks'. Paul was the founding Editor-in-Chief of Home News Magazine. He was also a recipient of Nigerian National Productivity Merit Award in Lagos, and winner of the Championship Awards. Paul holds postgraduate degrees in Business Administration and Organizational Leadership. King Paul, as fondly called is currently the President/CEO of Champion Insurance Services Inc, St Paul, Minnesota, USA.

INTRODUCTION

This book is directly focussed at re-inventing managers into full-proof icons of identifiable performance and concrete successes, who are ultimately permanently separated from poverty. While it could be said that this book teaches one how to be a highly performing manager; one could also say it shows how to move from poor life into wealthy living. Both goals are absolutely possible.

Every piece on the issues treated in the following pages is an impeccable fact; and being factual, will be thought-provoking and down-to-earth, practically relevant to you, the reader. In other words, you have a definite choice to make: either be angry enough to jettison this book now, or swallow your pride today to be rich and noble tomorrow. Indeed you will be glad to discover yourself as a top performer and a toast of Employers.

The discussions here address the forgotten side of managerial performance in the simplest form. By experience, I have discovered that while all Managers are faced with ability-based questions, most that can perform are bothered by questions that are delivery-based. In other words, you can do what you were asked to do but you don't know how best to do it. The five pronged wings of a star is the simplest graphical analogy of a managerial status and ideals associated with it. These are not taught in the Business Schools, yet they constitute the inter-play upon which a managerial success is predicated. You could call it "the other side of the manager," explaining why this advice manual has been intentionally kept simple and far from rigorous complexities common to academic exercises.

Managers Must Perform stems from a deep concern for the unfolding generation of workers who could achieve tremendous feats and rise through the ranks. Many of them have been kept below the poverty level, even though they could rise above it. Their parents inherited little or nothing and bequeathed same; they left them with no iota of nobility or relief from the pangs and clutches of poverty. The children also arrived from nothing sailing towards nowhere. A summary of their generational history is fast becoming the footprints of the wretched. They were raised broken and worked under heights of depression and poor attitudinal approach to duty.

Unfortunately, employers often recruit, based on sighting the certificates. They make judgement about skills or potential ability, but might not bother about the personality since they have little to confirm such credentials. It becomes a game of suspicion, and probation for the employer.

For the Manager, the probationary period is an easy ride; it passes by so soon, and could be well managed. The onus is on the Manager to re-orientate himself, with intentions beyond keeping the job; with a clear vision to perform and be a success, and thereby depart from the previous pattern. The Manager must break the generational jinx-- and that as fast as he could-- or else, he will end up like his predecessors. One is grieved by the sight of the young ones who suffer in the midst of plenty; who see available opportunities yet couldn't utilize them; whose privileges are withdrawn for reasons of birth and inclinations; whose prospects of gold mining is sharply dim; who are faced with little problems yet couldn't solve them, because they are poor; whose chances of coming to limelight were denied due to abject poverty. For such folks, the situation becomes a general resignation to fate because their immeasurable efforts to turn the tide had failed. This book will throw fog lights at such situations with a view to renewing hope and challenges.

This book runs a discourse on appropriate issues that would enable the reader become a better performer. As a manager, entrepreneur, self-made career person in the firm seeking to excel, the gold lines will help to ignite and propel you to an achiever. You can be a star. A star manager; A celebrity!

Being a star is a power game, hence this book offers a discrete discussion on power. The significance of enterprise performance as a parameter for success is discussed in analytical detail, and the concept of personality and principle is examined from a socio-psychological perspective. Quite exciting is the discourse on prosperity; in fact, a complete dose for a willing star is branded and packaged in this book.

Remember that these understandings shared are **extremely controversial** but shared in all sincerity to inspire you to **dig out the gold in you**. If I shirk from sharing this piece, many generations will be comprised of impoverished under achievers. You might feel slighted, but you will be happier for it! Be a Top Performer NOW!

Never choose to be Poor

You have to change your perspective about poverty as you know it. Your mind must first conclude that poverty was not a choice you made and you are willing to escape it when opportunities surface. Sometimes, people unconsciously choose to be poor. It is exhibited in the pattern of life they live.

You cannot afford to be poor, No never. To be poor is synonymous with 'to lack'. He lacks care. He lacks money. He lacks good friends. He lacks good health. He lacks good accommodation. He lacks sound and sufficient education. He lacks ability. He lacks good vision for the future. He lacks appeals. The life of the poor is a display of insufficiency in so many respects. They lack basic necessities for daily sustenance and proper survival; not because the necessities are not available, but because they are not affordable. The poor goes for the cheapest of goods, which though much in quantity, are the least in quality. They live under the 'manage, manage syndrome'. The poor can neither bark nor bite.

> **Resolution: Get out of Poverty!**

Make Profit
Poor people don't give. Not because they don't want to, but because they either don't have,

or for fear of losing the little they had. Often times, they hate to hear, or see, givers ask them for gifts. They resent hearing who gave what and why. Consequently, they break supernatural laws to gain by giving, since giving first occurred in the heart, transmitted to the head and conveyed in open hands. Giving encourages one to seek further rooms to make profit and thereby give more to expanding channels. But the poor do not seek profit because they think profit is not coming. It's a mind-set that requires a pill. The rich always seek to profit from all their labors.

Let the need to profit guide your decisions and actions. Never engage in whatever is not profitable. Your judgement as a Manager must be profit inclined. You will get a multiplier effect of such a mind-set as you will be propelled by a profit motive and discard negatives.

Poverty does not benefit the offspring and succeeding generations; and goes against the injunction of the Scriptures that 'a good man leaves an inheritance for his children'.

Though true, it may be difficult to accept that the poor are more arrogant than the rich. The African culture considers a man who has never tasted wealth as possessing a 'grab-all' tendency as soon as an opportunity presents itself. But one who had experienced wealth acts quite matured, because he/she is familiar to riches. In some cases, the poor are often afraid of asking for help because of this kind of ego. They resign themselves to fate, luck, destiny and false pretences. They sometimes feel slighted when offers are thrown at them without solicitation (by the rich. The reason is not farfetched – a good giver is a good receiver. Only the rich receives gifts with gladness.

> **Arrest poverty with all authority at your disposal**

Of Privileges and Rights

It is disheartening to be poor. The privileges of the poor are often denied and their rights severally trampled upon. There is no gainsaying the fact that injustice does exist all over the world, particularly in the developing economies. For example, a poor man in Africa has privileges and rights that may never be accorded him. While the rich is treated with civility, the poor man is beaten, battered, broken and coerced without dignity and for no reason.

He could be told that a privilege is not a right and thus should not be compelled when not offered. In the same breath, he could be informed that, if he feels his rights have been infringed upon, he should go to a court of law to seek redress. Since a poor man could not afford litigation fees and other associated expenses, what does the fellow do? He withdraws, 'goes solo' and resigns to fate. This is the trend, even in advanced economies. Folks without the wherewithal suffer a great deal of injustice more than those who have. A US Senator recently confirms that the poor are often put in jail, even for contestable offenses, because they lack the means to seek redress. Without prejudice, how many poor folks have been accorded demeaning responses, ignominious looks and disdainful treatments even where they ask for answers to legitimate questions? The poor are detested and molested. Their comments are rebuffed and their questions unanswered. But let a rich man walk in; he is offered a seat, given undivided attention and his reasonable and unreasonable questions are answered in a jiffy. An African adage rightly notes that, 'he who is rich has many relations but no one is a friend to a beggar'. I once went to a dealer's office to get my goods transported to my address. Dressed like a struggling dude, I was not warmly received and the uncertainty in the air matched the tone with which I was told 'if possible'. After a few days, I returned to the same place, meeting similar crowded situation; but now in a full corporate dress. I was surprised that an attention was instantly accorded to me, and a vehicle was ordered to deliver my goods 'unfailingly'. May be a confirmation of the way you dress, is the way you are addressed!

**Be poised, fully poised,
never to be poor**

Check out the Airports, there is a VIP lounge. Then ask for how many poor fellows have ever been offered a space at the VIP lounge. A poor man is not invited to such occasions where serious considerations and decisions are drawn to bear outstanding multiplier effect on life and living in the polity.

Furthermore, both the Bar and the Bench exist to sustain the long-held principle of equality before the law; a fact that may be normative, but is far from empirical. This is what should, but not what actually, operates. There is a world of difference between what should and what is. In our world, full equality before the law is not yet achieved. The poor and the rich are not yet equal before the law. There could be different outcomes for similar cases, depending on the pool of lawyers. The poor are not offered due privileges, nor have they the avenues to fully actualise their fundamental rights, either because those rights are not yet considered fundamental enough, or he does not know.

Parental Service

You must be poised to cross the borderline of poverty because you cannot afford to be a poor parent. To die wretched is a disservice to your children and wards. Raising children requires a lot of expense that the poor do not have. Poor children suffer unjustly and are denied without apology. Several basic necessities are not provided. They learn the language of scarcity and impoverishment too early in life. Some socio-psychological studies have proved that significant relationship exist between a number of social vices exhibited by youths, and their poor backgrounds. Thence they whip up resentment, fear, and hatred. Not only that; they exhibit care-free attitudes, they steal, are socially awkward due to lack of exposure, have the tendency to be violent, and grow up as juvenile delinquents, unleashing ills on their communities.

Proper and adequate parenting is expensive, yet a necessary luxury.

In view of the foregoing, I will show you the path to irreversible progress.

Chapter 1

POWER

Power is definitely transient, yet it provides an ultimate room for maximum service to God and optimum service to men. As a manager, you have power. The organization accorded you power to achieve result, not for personal aggrandisement. Your ability spells power; so does your position, but your power begins to diminish when you fail to deliver result. A manager's presence is power and it is contagious to achieve result if you know how to use it. Machiavelli noted that "He who wishes to be obeyed must know how to command." If you do not know how to use your managerial power, you are on the verge of failure.

Organizations are not like Santa Claus; they don't make managers because they 'like' people. They make managers from those who could deliver results. Making a manager is what the firm does. Getting the job done is your real deal, your end of the bargain. You make it, you keep it. You fail, you lose it. You lose power and privilege that can change your life and generation forever.

Organizations don't like people (at least primarily); they like profit. That is their benchmark. Period! Organizations don't like rhetoric, they shoot for result. If you deliver, period to period, they show you a path to more success, and give you more of their profit. Then you could wisely channel your direction out of poverty forever.

You probably think, organizations are mean Shylocks, always asking for a 'pound of flesh'. The truth is that, sometimes they are; in the real world. More often than not, organizations don't have to understand or care about the nitty-gritty of how you get the job done. They care about you getting the job done. That is why they made you a manager.

Managerial Appointments

I did stir up discussions about the need to differentiate between eligibility and suitability to management positions. The crux of my opinion was that because a manager was prima facie eligible to a position does not make him suitable for it. We can debate this position all day long. However, let me note that this position does not repudiate the need to ensure that parameters for the appointment of managers are well set and checked off the list. For example, where a position requires a degree, all degree holders may not be suitable for that appointment. The beauty of this is that a number of aptitude tests, pre-employment events, and psycho analytical test had been developed to help in this area.

Suffice it to stress that managers who seek appointment to such positions, should be cork sure that they are not only eligible for the job, but suitable for it as well; otherwise, the experience might be the most frustrating adventure you might have.

The Manager and Power

You probably wonder, what is the relationship between the manager and the seizure of power? There are two reasons for this intersection: the company's job is to choose the manager who will deliver and the manager's job is to pursue an emancipation route from poverty. The reason for the latter is just because the manager is not a volunteer. While the company wants to achieve its goal, you want to be paid, and get ahead with the result of your success. If it's not your grandfathers' company, then you don't own it. The day the Will is read, the chief slave will come to the reality of his status. Be the manager who delivers to expectation and use that success pedestal to seize power, and ultimately wealth. That's it, period! It is like a mutual symbiotic benefit in play between the company and the manager.

Thus, for effective application of power, you must be good, very good at what you do. Distribute assignment without looking back. The onus for result is on your tail, so be sure you can get expected result. Your organization have little concern about your employees, they bother about you. And you must deliver result!

As a manager, you need to understand power. I will compare it in relation to the poor for ease of understanding. While the poor repudiates power, the rich treasures it and long after it. Where the poor dream of holding the reins of power, he treads only in a fantasy island because he does not know the content of power, the use of power, and the consolidation of power. The poor cannot pay the cost of acquiring power because it is expensive, very expensive. Power to the poor is a strange-sum game. Power to the poor is a mystery wrapped up in a lidless cocoon, with a transparent content but an undefined open end. Those who gained power never merely asked for it, never merely bargained for it, never merely offered a price for it, and never simply had it as a gift. Those who gained power simply **seized it.**

> While the Poor repudiates power, the Rich treasures it.
> Dream the seizure of power!

That's why we refer to <u>Seizure of Power</u> to depict how power is acquired. Power itself never sought to be acquired. It rides on the pendulum, available only to those who seized it.
Name it:

Political power ⎫
Charismatic power ⎪
Intellectual power ⎪
Legal power ⎪
Financial power ⎬ those who possessed
Military power ⎪ it actually seized
Civil power it. ⎪
Information power ⎪
Religious power ⎭

To possess any of the foregoing, you have to conquer both competitors and contenders, failure to which you cannot acquire power. These terrains do not permit the poor to have an inch hold whatsoever, as their compelling circumstances do not adequately cater for the requirements of advancing to seize power. Yet, you need power to be rich or when you are rich, you need power to sustain and consolidate it. And remember, your ultimate goal was to succeed and create wealth as a manager whose future will be the beginning of new generation.

Let me analyze your organization for you:
You must never take up a Managerial appointment until you understand your organization.
You must understand the organizational complexities and deal with it accordingly to succeed in it.

Power Cabal

These are radical, moderate and conservative. Your organization is made up of these. Members can belong to either of the camps. This point elucidates the relationship between the powerful and the wealthy, and the force behind your organization. For you to succeed, you must understand how they operate and for what reasons. It describes the fact that a small group, or clique, or cabal actually holds control over the wealth of nations, either as persons, group of persons or organizations.

This Cabal however has 3-pronged ideological philosophies which does not, in the ultimate, jeopardize their prime concord. For example, the wealth cabal is the same as the power cabal. Its prime conclusion and unity of direction is in the consolidation of wealth, the furtherance of wealth and the use of power.

The following are the ideological beliefs of each of the parties of the Cabal:

1. **Totalitarian Radicals**
Membership-Admission is prohibited in this group. No admittance. Wealth Application is towards totality in control of men and materials.

The Totalitarian-Radical believes that nobody else should be allowed to become as rich as they were hence they discourage admission into membership of the Cabal. It's like reaching the heights only to pull the ladder to oneself to ensure no one else climbs.

This group has no interest in your climbing the ladder. No matter what you do, you can't go beyond what has been prescribed for you. Expect no better reward from them. In such organizations, achieve success only as a stepping stone to move forward. Don't waste your life there by claiming loyalty, counting years, and winning long service awards. If the totalitarian radicals dominate your organization, you must keep your eyes open for other opportunities.

2. **Totalitarian Moderate**

Membership-admission is allowed but extremely restricted. It is like the proverbial camel passing through the eye of a needle. Wealth Application is slightly bent, occasionally to be humane, without jeopardising the ulterior totalitarian motive.

On the other hand, the Totalitarian-Moderate encourages admission (i.e. others becoming as rich as they were) but under very stringent rules and conditions that are extremely difficult to accomplish. This indicates that those who qualify are eventually few and indeed very few. To them, the pathway to wealth, though tortuously long and rough, is possible. If this class run your organization, your hard work will pay later. You have to be very convincing, and they will let you on board.

3. __The Conservatives__

They do not hold extreme appeal to Membership-admission and wealth applications. Anyone who succeeds at seizure of wealth and or power (whichever comes first) should be so admitted into the Cabal while the use of wealth should be its re-investment into the men, the polity and the organization for developmental advantages. They are the rich but are philanthropic. They are rich, very rich; they know so, but they share it.

The Conservatives (not totalitarian-conservative as above) believe that anyone who wishes to be admitted into membership is so obliged and assisted to be as rich as others. They also believe that their wealth could be ploughed back into societal development, to the advantage of some (who meet standards) thus making way for others to be rich. They do not see their wealth or control of power as being threatened; to them, the sky is wide enough for all stars to shine. Perhaps this class could be called 'compassionate conservatism' (borrowing a word from President George W. Bush). If you are a manager here, your efforts and achievement could propel you to great heights.

4. Common Grounds

For the sake of clarity, the cabal in control of wealth and power agree that:

- they must retain the control;
- they must expand their wealth base and;
- they must use it to seize and utilize power.

The differences arrive at the paths to which anyone else can join them i.e. become wealthy. They also differ on how they use or employ their wealth and power.

Call it controversial:
Every Wealthy Man in our Society falls under
one of the Parties in the Cabal.

Some of the parties explained above could have so arrived due to various reasons, experiences and circumstances of their lives. In the cabal therefore:

- Some cannot see others wealthy; they do not permit it;
- Some don't wish others wealthy but if some achieved it, they live with it;

- Some hope, plan and work to see others wealthy and make instruments available to so do.

It would be an undue dissipation of mental capacity to shirk away from these truths. Several reasons however exist for every line of position.

How they Became Rich

There are 3 ways to get power or wealth:
- ✓ By Privilege
- ✓ By Communal Support
- ✓ By Hardwork ⟶ self- made men

Privilege

There are wealthy men or women who did arrive by privilege. They inherited the instruments of prosperity and built on them. Their parents or guardians had laboured to acquire enormous resources, which had become the basis of their achievements. They had a stepping-stone on which they make further progresses. For example, some legal luminaries have had their legal world inherited by their children. Same goes for family-owned businesses that had grown into multi-national corporations.

Communal Support

There are other people who were not born rich, or with silver spoons in their mouths; but they were opportune to receive help and various forms of assistance from relations, community, friends, acquaintances and the state, which aided them to achieve laudable successes in life. This category comprise of those whose progress in life could have been virtually impossible were it not for mental, material and perhaps, spiritual assistance received from their associates or helpers.

Hard Work ⟶ Self-Made Men

There are other great ones who had had no inheritance or assistance except from their own hands. They had nobody but themselves. They had no inheritance solid enough to launch them into progressive beginning. Without choice or help, they pursued their dreams. They feel absolutely responsible for their joy and success. Whatever they had achieved was by dint of hard work on their part.

In essence and comparisons therefore, those who feel that the aristocratic domination of wealth-power and its distribution should be an exclusively guarded terrain, would not wish to

28

allow others to enter. Others who consider their heights of attainment, as mere privilege of fate and sheer grace of the heavens, would not object to others who want to reach similar heights.

Consequently, the onus of decision falls on you who intend to be rich and possess wealth. You can be rich, and that, definitely! The facts however are clear that it might not be a rosy lick of a chocolate candy but a rugged, never-say-die-determination to go high up and succeed. It also connotes that there are rooms for making it to the cabal and **you can, if you think that you can. You can because you really can.**

You can join them–Decide to do!

I once wrote the story of two proverbial birds (here named Tully and Tally) locked up in a cage by their Captor. They were both provided with food and water. The Mother Bird occasionally visited both and they recounted their ordeals as follows:

Tully : (Bird 1) – "I awoke each day to regret my life captured by the fists of a wicked man who denies me the glorious experience of flying through the winds and perching at the peak of trees. My food is bitter and my drink is sour. This is my twenty-fifth day."

Tally: (Bird 2) – "I awoke each day to find my food and drink supplied. My Captor is my servant and guard, both day and night providing me with all I am looking for while flying through the peaks and winds. My food is sweet and collected in bowls with a drink. I cannot remember how long I've been in this snare, but I hope for many more days living like a princess"

The Mother bird wrote a sentence to each of them. To the first, *'Your death is in your eye'*. To the other, *'Your life is in your eye'*. While the former was found dead one morning, the second became adapted as a homely pet bird. From all indications, the perception of the mind matters indeed.

Everyone is created with great ingenuity. It takes the right eye to discover oneself and discover others. You must first believe in yourself before you do others. You may not be able to do everything, but you can do something; and that, very uniquely. It has been scientifically proven that fingerprints of two individuals are never exactly alike; even twins hold distinct personalities. *You are never me, I am never you. You are you, I am me. I don't have to be you because it makes me a copy of you and a 2nd best. I am worse if you are also a copy of another. Just let me be me. It's the best for me.* You are unique in your own right and very exceptional in personality, purpose and pursuits.

The feats by folks like Thomas Edison, Serena & Venus Williams, Bill Gates, Oprah Winfrey; Warren Buffet, Michael Jordan, Albert Einstein, Steve Jobs, Jerry Yang, Martin Luther King, and Tiger Woods among others, are predicated upon their conviction that they could achieve the impossible. They overcame the odds and surged forward to do marvellous things. The difference between achievers and others is that while the former kept overcoming the odds, the latter backpedalled and withdrew. Everyone will be a manager, if everyone could do what the manager does.

> **It is not only possible to dine with the Stars**
> **It is also possible to shine as Stars**
> **Get ready to Shine!**

Chapter 2

PERFORMANCE

Be Good at Duty Post

God does not usurp your own responsibilities. God who gave men gifts, talents and orientations, did confirm that 'a man's gift will make room for him and bring him before great men' (Prov. 18:16). If God gave the gift, the gifted should sit up and be good to utilise the gift. Prove that you are one of the best in your area of duty. It could go a long way to make you succeed. You may never know where your ability would be discussed and judgements either in favour or against passed on you. Whatever you intend to do or do, decide to be gold, no less! While you aim at the Everest, you might land on Kilimanjaro Mount.

2.   Of Managers and Leading

It would be difficult to be a manager if you are poor. I have led over 14 groups with some having very extensive impact across people and communities. It is hard to lead if you are poor. It behoves me to observe that even the heavens raise up the poor before making him a leader. Heaven makes provision for every vision that is commissioned. Whoever has not accomplished somewhere cannot perform elsewhere.

The process of leadership selection is anti-poor. It provides no room for the enlistment of the downtrodden. The poor is unnoticed and his status unrecognised. In fact, the vote of the poor is circumvented as he is offered a pool of selections from which to elect his choice. He cannot take the ultimate decision alone; his is not a choice per se, but a guarded and guided selection.

Who is a leader anyway?

A leader is one who conveys influence over another. Does a poor man bear such an influence? A city joke says, when a rich man is giving a speech, the poor does not pose an idea. If he does, no one will buy it. The views of the poor are not heard. When heard, they are not heeded. When heeded, they are not ascribed to the poor. Many of the quoted words on marble today were authored by the rich, or in the least, the comfortable. It was only in the 17th Century that poor men were ever quoted or heard, and perhaps, not any longer. Even those quoted then were educated and influential.

Through the generations, the poor do not make decisions or lead, except through violent demonstrations, civil disobedience, and uprisings, which had compelled a change. Those changes were in fact, made possible by the rich who are fair minded and willing to concede some grounds. For example, abolition of slavery might not have been possible if some noble folks in the chambers of power had not supported it. The poor fights the battle but the rich savours the victory. The choice of the leader has never been given to the poor. The leader thus chosen, often separates from their original (low) class and commune with the upper class. They sing different songs and offer tokens to pacify the poor and entrench the 'divide and rule' syndrome. The greatest irony of this is that, the poor themselves do not choose the least of the poor or their likes to lead them. An adage warns: "Do not make a wretch, the guard of a treasury."They often prefer the rich to do so and justify their stand. Sociologically, a poor fellow is never made a group's treasurer. The poor only have their say, the rich have their way. The poor advise while the rich decide.

> **To Join Decision Makers, Be Rich**

In many nations, leadership is entrusted into the hands of a cabal consisting of a few rich fellows. The primary prerequisite is the possession of wealth. Even local groups and small entities choose their leaders by the same parameters.

Leadership is expensive, only the rich can afford it. Leadership connotes: exposures, etiquette, appearance, decorum, language, dexterity, mobility, communication, personality, qualifications, healthiness, influence, associations, affiliations, intelligence etc.

The ability to garner them is wealth. The poor needs that terrain to lead.

Decide to get there!

---

3. **Managers do not make Excuses**

Excuses make men poor. Everyone who succeeds has an excuse that could have been tabled as a hindrance for each action taken. There can be no acceptable excuse for complacency.
Organizations avoid, actually detest, managers who make excuses. Where excuses are not avoided and valid visions pursued, they would

cage your mind and impoverish your hands. In fact, *the sluggard will not plough by reason of the cold; therefore shall he beg in harvest and have nothing* (Prov. 20:4). It needs be added that weaklings, especially those who make themselves such, can never be successful. Sometimes, work must be done at night to achieve target. It is a refreshing period for meditation too. Give up excuses, especially on the basis that neither men nor things could alter before you act. For example, how does one posit that he could have made it successfully had he been born elsewhere? Such unfounded excuses should be thrown overboard, because, the fact is clear that he wasn't born there. I mean, every successful person has reasons why he should not have succeeded. There is no achiever that did not cross and conquer a hurdle. One should settle down with transparent facts before him and face the challenges, as they appear, not on wishes.

4. **Managers and Priorities**

Generally, everyone can have a scale of preference. You choose according to the order of significance because you cannot afford every item on your scale. When the chips are actually down, the poor does not list or observe priorities. For example a list of the wishes or desires of a poor man differs from his priority list. If by mistake, he converts his wishes to his list of priorities, he soon discovers that he's only building 'castles in the air' and embarking on a frivolous mission. The reason stem from the fact that, he does not have the ability to actualise the dream.

The priorities of a rich man are dictated by time. He carries the ability to perform. He carries the ability to actualise the dream. Ask King Solomon for his scale of preference, he'll declare: *whatever my heart desires, I withheld not from it*. The rule was – see it done, call it delivered.

It is the inability to satisfy wants that compel the poor to make strenuous choices among few things.

> **You must have a priority list per time, per project**

5.   **Be Meticulous**

You must be meticulous, carefully checking up details of documents, materials, information, proposals, etc. I've had a privilege to work with many people, several of whom are unduly in a hurry. They do not care for details about what catches their attention. If that is not your strength, then find someone to double-up for your inadequacy. A great man does not append his signature on anything until carefully scrutinized. I met a man who processed an affidavit on which his typist had typed for him a wrong date of birth. Another fellow had her name and title misspelt on her affidavit. These were expensive laxities that could lead to extensive damages. The faculties of the head should be employed to serve its purposes.

Entries should be checked, records kept, letters edited and proposals proofread as much as possible to make your document error-proof. For example, if you omit the word 'NOT' in a text, you could in entirety misrepresent motive or content and cause irreparable mistakes to your discourse.

6.   **Find Knowledge**
     More often than not, managers forget that they have two ears and one mouth. They should listen more than talking. Listening and learning charge your brain battery. Wisdom is imparted but knowledge is found out. In every area of pursuit, you must dig out every available information on what you intend to do, in order to

do it well. Books are immeasurable treasures; they could leave a person better informed. To buy a castle, I would recommend that you first buy a book. The first day of your appointment as a manager, choose two books: one about yourself, and the other about your organization.

You have to reinvent yourself, or you are doomed to fail. Actually, organizations should handover two books to managers they appoint, within the first week of their appointment. Wisdom is indeed the principal thing and with all our getting, get understanding (the Scripture). Wisdom is profitable to direct. Knowledge directs the application of wisdom. To know what to do is wisdom; to know how to do it is knowledge; to do it the way it should be done is efficiency, and to do it acceptably is service. Knowledge makes a man better than his peers.

Ideas make men
Information makes the nations

Ideas make men, information makes the nations. Don't just dream, get informed and get well informed about what you want to pursue. Nobody becomes a medical practitioner without having acquired the prerequisite knowledge. You can wish and desire till tomorrow to be anything but mere desires don't make people. If wishes were horses, men will ride them to death.

Get a working knowledge, and any kind of knowledge which actually works. We live in an age where there is access to an immeasurable array of information. You can get to know so much by the touch of a finger; so there is no excuse for anyone who needed to know and could not. Sources of great and startling information have increased, providing unique opportunities to know what, where, how, when and who. You can only perform to the level of your knowledge. The Press, the Internet, the Libraries, Books, Journals/Magazine/Periodicals, Dailies, Leaflets, Telephone, Fax, Records, Archives, Tertiary Institutions, Public Affairs Commentators, Documentaries, Television programmes, Data Banks, Bill Boards, Advertorials, are various sources of useful information, etc. It is knowledge that provokes knowledge.

To sum this further, **listening** and **learning** definitely charge up your brain battery. No matter who, or what, you are, every inch of your progress and success is determined by

(a)   how much you know
(b)   how much of what you know is
*   employed or put to use; and*
(c)   *how much of what you know*
        actually works.

It is regrettable that in our part of the world, people communicate and listen to a huge pot of junks, which does no good. A properly directed individual should listen more, learn much and say little. One progresses by the level of one's knowledge. Your transformation is only limited by the extent of information available to you. It's not possible to be where you have not seen; and it is impossible for you to see what you have not sought. You cannot see what you haven't heard about. The unknown cannot make impact. It's got to be known first, then it's useful. Thus, every iota of knowledge used, requires a refill and replenishment; in fact, a progressive re-fill, which is gained by listening and learning. We've got to listen to people, the circumstances around our hearts, our heads and others. What you should do with acquired knowledge is explained hereafter. When the learning has taken place, you are better positioned for better performance. There is no manager that can deliver expected result with a high degree of nonchalant mediocrity. No one actually performs beyond the measure of information available to him. Charge up your life by: getting information; acquiring knowledge; and learning through them.

> **You cannot perform beyond the level of information available to you**

7. **Hard work**

Good thinkers are good over-takers. Over-takers work hard, eventually becoming groundbreakers. There can be no lasting success on a platter of ease. If you fail in the days of adversity, (says Holy Scripture) your strength is small. Those who arrived at the thresholds of history are those whose hands laboured hard. The greatest of men who proved themselves in the day were awake while their colleagues slept at nights. World histories have lauded credence to the fact that those who 'carried the day' are those who burnt 'candles at night'. Hence, to carry the day, just candle the night.

Those who carried the day, burnt candles at nights

There seems to be no short cut. Whoever dreams of soaring heights, yet laced with ineptitude, laziness, and impoverishing idleness, will only be honoured at last with good idea but poor inventions, a great fellow who did nothing. They constitute the negativities of the world. The Scriptures clarify that he who works his land will have abundant food; but he who chases fantasies lacks judgement, the work of his hand rewards him. This is because wealth gathered by labour shall increase (Prov. 12:11, 14; 13:11). Hard work is not in terms of spending time at a working place; it is how much you could achieve within a reasonable time frame. It is sometimes, not how far, but how well. Both divestment and investment consume time, but only investment yields result. Every divestment must be re-invested to reap good result.

> Both divestment and investment consume time but only investment yields result

43

In fact, investment produces achievement. Nothing guarantees the future of a man like his investments. It is a crystal clear law of nature. Sowing brings reaping. You don't sow, you can't reap; period! I mean good investments in real estates and the capital market. With good ideas, you can't lose on these fronts. World billionaires had arrived via these paths: solid investment in stocks and real estates. If you ever make money through remuneration, re-invest some part of it in those areas. This will give you lasting resources.

The most returns you could get, come from manufacturing. The percentage of returns in manufacturing business could be over 30%, while your returns elsewhere could be less. If you have an idea, create something; sell your creation, and reap the benefit in sales. You must plan when next you change your status from employee to employer. Bank interests can't yield as much as these lines of investments. If you are scared of investing, leave your money in deposits. It might crawl, but it will grow.

You are not expected to spend away your hours, but invest them in quality activities which could contribute to the ultimate goal. It is not mere working longer in most cases, but working smarter. Whoever spends 8hrs at work as a globetrotter, differs from one who invested quality 8hrs of measurable productivity. In several organizations, workers while away time in many ways.

A great team is a unique asset to any manager, and you must be able to adapt to different people and personalities to exact your maximum effect. It was Zig Ziglar who wrote 'leaders who are dynamic understand that they need fluidity in their style of leadership, so as to be able to get along with everyone. Leadership involves getting along with, and getting maximum production from, everyone, including those with whom we disagree. This flexibility is what dynamic leaders possess that allows them to guide their teams through both good times and the tough ones.'[3]

Managers can't do or work like their employees. You have to be smarter than your team, or you lose both power and control. Never lose control of your group or you are done. If your group or team is 'hijacked' by your employee, you must act accordingly. Your next line of action could include: deployment, firing, removal, suspension, or rendering redundant; until you are back in charge.

Corporate executive don't give much cognizance to employees, they care about the manager. Who cares about the late, *waka-about* (i.e. merry-go-round) and funny employees, or the self-appointed grapevine leader? If the manager is delivering result, anybody else can do whatever they like. There is no executive that wants to be your grandmother or babysitter, though they may never tell you.

I propose the following formula for measuring hard work:

MMH–Minimum Measurement For Hard work

List all actions and inactions done through the day under the headings: plus and minus (+ -)

(a)   List 5 items of duty in the first 4hrs of work

(b)   List 5 items concluded in the last 4hrs of work

(c)   Compare the value of the 10 items in relation to ultimate target (Are they directly/indirectly related?)

(d) Measure time utilised for actions, viz: those not related to target and those related to target

(e) Assess (c) and (d)

(f) Draw fair conclusions.

Where a significant proportion of your time had been invested in the negative rather than the positive, it may be appropriate to conclude that you have wasted several useful efforts elsewhere. Hard work is a corroboration of many items, some of which have been treated under relevant sub-heads. Suffice it to agree that *if you cannot excel with talents, you can triumph with efforts.* Employ either or both for best yield.

For example: A Salesperson who had a target to sell 12 books on a particular day could distribute his /her priorities as stated below:

S/N	Actions	+ -	Time	Time used (8-10hrs available)
1.	Examine all received orders for purchase	+	8 -9.30a.m	1 1/2hrs
2.	Execute delivery of orders (15 orders)	-	-	-
3.	Deposits to Bank	-	-	
4.	Visited Clients	+	9.30 -12.30p.m	3hrs
5.	Discussed personal matters/Received visitors	+	12.30 -2.30p.m	2hrs
6.	Tenders for New Sales/Get sales lead	+	2.30-4.30p.m	2hrs
7.	Laundry	-		
8.	Post Ledgers	-	-	
9.	Preside over Staff Meeting	-		
10.	Social Activity	+	4.30-6.00p.m	1 1/2hrs

Key:

+   Action taken

-        Action not taken

Time invested in activities = 10hrs

Directly related to goal = $6_{1/2}$hrs

Not directly related to goal = $3_{1/2}$hrs

The judgement on time usage efficiency or performance is that of the individual. The nearest future (towards the end of the year) will determine if you had run a wasted year or not. An adage says there is no proxy treatment at the hospital.

48

Someone else cannot be treated for the ailment you have. You are responsible for yourself!

8.   Managers are 'can' people

When you were appointed, someone talked to somebody about your assumed ingenious ability to deliver results. They thought you could! How then did you think you could not? Think that you can. Say it loud: I can!!! No matter what you have ever been, or coming from you can! You can actually be the beginning of a new generation. If you fail, you have simply postponed the happy days of many (generations) coming right after you, who might have to start all over again. I know a millionaire today, who was once a salesman and a bicycle repairer until the opportunity to be a Dealer opened up. He actively responded and thereafter became a manufacturer of same set of products. A billionaire was reported to have once beaten drums and yet rose to become a world renowned business mogul. Believe in yourself! Your mind matters__ a great deal.

9.   **Take Risks**

Christopher   Columbus   discovered America.   He was initially faced with 'Ne plus ultra' *nothing more beyond*–like challenges but he plunged into the unknown to discover the chief of nations. Every great researcher had first treaded on the terrains of the unknown, and taken risks before their landmark discoveries. If only he had agreed that nothing more existed beyond the point he had reached, fate would have condemned him to the forgotten dust of history, never to be mentioned again. Anyone who disappoints destiny at an opportune point is always confined to the dust of history. Those who succeed at such appointments with destiny are not only written in gold, but also graven in sapphires stones; at least in the hearts of surviving generations, just like Columbus.

> **Whatever would make a man known as a Giant would primarily lie on the Unknown Rocks to be discovered by a Willing Mind**
> **Achievers are Risk Takers**

Take risks where compelling. Don't be threatened by it. *Achievers are Risk Takers.*

Ask for the experiences, circumstances and challenges of Eli Whitney, Thomas Edison, Henry Ford, Alexander Graham Bell, The Wright Brothers, Nicolaus Copernicus, Isaac Newton, Gregor Mendel, Albert Einstein, Charles Dickens, George Eliot, Leonardo da Vinci, Michelangelo, Saint Augustine, Martin Luther, Thomas Aquinas, Constantine the Great, George Washington, Abraham Lincoln, Mahatma Gandhi, Martin Luther King, Obafemi J. Awolowo, and the Great Zik of Africa. Majority of them had a humble beginning, but rode on their past to possess their present unforgettable heights. The world can never forget them in a hurry. Never ever! You are not the first to have a problem, and you are not the worst fellow around. Those who made it had bigger problems, which laced their shoes yet made giant strides with them!

10. Communicate what matters
a) **Say what matters**

Life serves different kinds of kettles. Many people are where they are because they talked. Others are there because they did not talk. Most problems arise because people talk junks – words of no value or worth. It is the beauty of an ear to hear, more and more, never dull of hearing. It is the honour of the eye to get the sight of much. But it is the duty of me and YOU to follow the noblest course and thereby, control what the instincts demand. For example, a man who aspires to great heights, need not share his dreams with every Tom, Dick and Harry; because not everybody is relevant to it.

For you to succeed as a manager, you must be able to communicate; both laterally, and horizontally. This piece is all over the managerial trainings. But then, whoever is not important to achieving your goal need not hear about it. Furthermore, there is no room for sentiments in managerial accomplishments. You have to fire your cousin if he or she becomes a clog in the wheel of progress. The firing has to be done smartly, so you could still have dinner together later that night. That is an empirical truth! If you don't know how to dismiss a non-beneficial parasitic friend, you will pay dearly for it soon. Leave sentiments out of managerial responsibilities.

If you share your dream with one who has no iota of impact on it, what do you gain? If nothing, why share it? Issues must be discussed where it matters; and if scientists were to be taken right, "matter is anything that has weight and occupies space". Thus, where no substance exists, matters of significance need not be discussed. Of what glory will it be for a man who published his **dreams** rather than his **discoveries**? Even Mary, in the midst of wonders *kept all these things, and pondered them in her heart* (Lk. 2:18).

b)   **Say What Matters to those who Matter**

No matter how hungry men are to hear the latest about you, talk only to those who matter. If you feel someone could assist to fulfil the vision, then talk to him or her. Where you have to knock, go ahead. Never fear that you could be rejected or treated disdainfully. The worst that could be meted out to you is to throw you out when the door is opened. But then, you may never predict the response to your request, **so make it**. If the response was pleasant – fine, if not thank God, turn your back and seek or knock elsewhere. The fact that a door was closed against you does not dictate that all doors will be. You might have miscalculated in your judgement, or arrived at an odd hour of the moment. No matter what, a favourable response exists somewhere! Not all listeners of adverts have heeded its persuasive plea but some will definitely do. So, the media will always have adverts!

c)   **Say What Matters, the way it Matters**

Be communication solid. No one buys a dream poorly conveyed. If you have something to sell, then you must speak well in choice words, make adequate contacts with reasonable dexterity and sell it. You will be carried in the way you call yourself. If you call yourself a King, the palace will be made accessible. If you call yourself a riffraff, men will lead you to the ghetto. If you call yourself a Nun, people will show you the monastery. If you are a salesman, people will look out for your wares. There is no buyer that wishes to willingly part with his money. As a manager, they expect you to manage. A buyer wants to be convinced that it is no regret parting with his money to buy your good or service. You must remember that the buyer has countless alternatives and several appeals. You must be good at it. Mediocrity does not sell anymore. You either do well or you back out of stage. The trend has grown fully competitive, hence only the best will make the landmarks.

11.   Quit When You Must

There are instances when it is in the best interest and decision of the manager to quit. I have heard folks regard those who threw in the towel as mediocre, weaklings, deserters, and so on; and in some cases they are right. The fact is you must quit, when you must quit!

In situations where your ability, ingenuity and resourcefulness are no longer trusted, it is a matter of time before you are fired under some kind of pretence. So, you could get out before someone ruin your noble records with one line of insanity. You don't have to keep fighting to hold on to what you will eventually lose; you might blame yourself. You could test the waters and feel the tempo around your peers, checking to see if the acceptance level had gone south and you are no longer considered useful or beneficial to the organization. It does not mean weakness or lack of a fighting spirit or tenacity, but prompt decisive action to leave and fight another day. An adage says he who fights and knows when to retreat, will live to fight another day.

When as a manager you see the handwriting on the wall telling you to quit, then you should. Don't wait until you are fired or

55

removed. The following are some of the tell-tale signs that you are no longer needed:

   i.   Changes made to your department without considering your input;

   ii.   You've been getting repeatedly written up for issues that may not warrant such outrageous lines of action;

   iii.   Your position had been threatened by board politics and/ or/ you discovered that you had been stripped of your legitimate departmental authority;

   iv.   You have been slammed with undeliverable and incoherent goals in a manner incompatible with the organizational pattern.

The foregoing and many more can be referred to as systematic frustration tactics deployed to get rid of you. You have to get out before it's too late. Don't wait to get fired, just Quit!

Chapter 3

THE MANAGERS' PERSONALITY

Get an Idea to Work

Managers work in the realm of ideas. The manager is the only one with the solemn duty to conceptualize. You must keep giving birth to, rolling out and testing ideas. Within your department, you are the breathing brain in action. Your brain can't sleep. Breakthroughs don't come from doing the same thing over and over. It comes from new initiatives. Initiatives about how things could be better achieved and how better things could become inventions. It is the managers' job to connect the dots, pull ideas of the team together to make a whole, and redirect everyone's efforts towards the feat. What you created in your imagination is the result of the product on the production floor. You are the brain! The manager's consistent quest is, what's the next idea?

Any ground breaker must first have an idea. An idea has an inherent value and a contagiously reproductive capacity to metamorphose into full-blown realities, with unique impact on people, places and issues. Idea evolves from an environment. An environment consists of information-carrying elements. This set the genius up to work. Whatever an idea is set to tackle: be it to solve a problem; create a new world or a new rebirth; transform a personality; relive a poser; accomplish a target; or perform a function; it has the capacity to achieve it. It was Umesh Ramakrishnan who quoted Bill Amelio (President/CEO of Lenovo) to have said "when I was in college, I was fascinated by the ability of leaders --from business to politics--to command attention, captivate people, and make them understand a vision"[1]There are actions or principles to be furthered on ideas; some of which are:

a)   **Search for Ideas**
      Ideas are to be sought. Wherever, whenever, however, whatever; ideas must be sought. You must never discard an idea before it is examined. There is nothing like a useless idea. An idea may only be inapplicable at a point in time. The power of the seed is inherent in it.

b)   **Sort Ideas**
All ideas may not be applicable to a particular problem but some could. Hence a neat sorting of available ideas should be done. Identify such ideas that are relevant and do correspond with the situation at hand.

c)   **Test Ideas**
Subject your ideas (applicable ones) to a well-defined test. In this case, you draw the path for the idea as to what you intend it to do at the end. Pose the ideas at some persons with appropriate experience on it and ask for responses. Verify what the outcome of those who had used such ideas had been. While this attempt does not give you conclusions, it enables you to have an avalanche of information at your disposal to analyse the pros and cons of the idea. You could however draw a hypothetical conclusion though not yet certified.

d)   **Solve Ideas**
In the course of testing your ideas, you come to realise that there are envisaged obstacles to seeing the full effect of such ideas. These obstacles are to be prepared for and attended to accordingly. There is no idea that does not attract

some form of hitches along with it and every good idea will face its own bottlenecks be it at initiation/incubation, development, emancipation or implementation stage. The import here is that one should be ready to tackle obstacles envisaged or apparently facing the idea.

e)   **Work Ideas: Ideas grow feet and wings**
Ideas are values waiting for valiant to discover but they are nothing in themselves until actualised. The composite value of an idea is not explicit until proven and effected. Anybody can dream to be anything, but what he eventually becomes is the substance of the dream, and what he or she does with it.

You must thus work out your idea. This is definitely the hardest aspect of working to see an idea come true. Issues and challenges will appear not as imaginations, but as facts; not as thoughts, but as realities. Yet, you must keep the vision bright, dream alive and the idea on line, no matter what.

I believe the thought that *those who sit, yearn; those who sleep, dream; those who walk, see vision; those who see visions, run; those who run, achieve; those who achieve, are go-getters; go-getters are leaders.*

There is nothing like failing to see an idea come to reality. The worst that could surface is that you couldn't actualize the idea, because a better idea realisable appeared. You can never fail putting an idea to work. However, where the guidelines are followed, it is largely possible that the proposed idea will work out.

> **You are not a moron**
> **Get an idea! Make it work!!**
> **Make it Work for You!!!**

2.   Build Itineraries

No manager succeeds without well-cut itineraries. Lack of itinerary, is a characteristic of poverty. Poverty remains a hydra-headed virus that inflicts a potent damage on several facets of life. Among these is the itinerary of the poor. It is regrettable but factual, that the poor do not have a daily itinerary that could be drawn, compelled and completed. Where drawn (perhaps intuitively), any intervening element that promotes either perquisites or fear immediately alters the itinerary. Any plan to perform an action by the poor can be altered simpli cita. The reasons

61

include variables that lend credence to the effectual performance of a daily/weekly/monthly/annual programme of action. Since a plan is a proposed course of action or direction, it connotes that it was yet to be achieved. It thus means that there are requirements to its accomplishment. Such requirements are multi-various and are largely not in the terrain of the ability of the poor.

Suppose a man had an appointment to negotiate for a job at a distance of 50km from his residence? As simple as that was, he would need, among other prerequisites: a well-ironed outfit ready for use; an undisturbed early rise; a means of transportation (a reasonably prestigious arrival is an added advantage to securing favourable treatment), sufficient amount of money for incidentals; a means of communication before and after negotiation; a commanding language, coupled with appreciable disposition and persuasion; and acceptable standard of documental presentations etc. It would be costly for the poor to meet up. Sudden influences to which he is subjected could dissuade him. His presentations could be far below expectations. His appearance might be unappealing, and his communication most repudiating. Take it or leave it; there is a language of the poor and a language of the rich. Some of these constitute a disadvantage to the poor.

3.   The Poor and Partners

An adage says *no one is related to the poor but everyone is a kinsman of the rich.* If you are rich, your relations are many and scattered. If you are poor, even your relations might deny knowing you; after all, what is the benefit of being a cousin to a pauper except misery, sadness and face capping. Proverbs abound that *the poor is hated even of his own neighbour but the rich has many friends* (Prov. 14:20).

Even the poor don't befriend themselves. They have more delight in being friends of the wealthy. Sharing is indeed sour where one party lacks. Truly, it does not pay the poor to be his fellow's friend, why and for what gains?

In fact, where the rich attempt to befriend the poor, it is often engulfed in misconceptions as the poor doubt the rich, querying the intentions behind such an adventure. Very, very few poor men bear the courage to dare befriend the rich.

4.
Get on Boat, Sail out of Poverty now! Friends will then naturally unfold!

He who stands alone will soon be tired of loneliness. Everyone should associate with another because fortunes are not built single-handedly neither is it enjoyed single-handedly. The reality of life has posited that **friends make fortune for friends**. Thus, one must associate with those that matter. Not necessarily those that matter in resources such as money, but particularly those that matter in mind, in skill, in exposure, in intelligence, in purpose, in focus and of course in substance. Associate with those who are better than you, and you will be better off.

> **Be pleasant to all, fair to many, good to some and special to few**

Any friend whose association to your life does not carry an iota of value should be dumped and discarded. Managers do not have the luxury of priests. By the luxury of priests, I mean the longsuffering, patience, simplicity, sacrifice, desire not to offend a parishioner, abstinence, and a seventy times seven forgiveness of a crude costly offender. Managers' role is dictated by profit and not humanitarian gestures.

Furthermore, no manager is expected to change his role to that of a priest at the confessional when decisions that directly affect results are on the line. It is a naïve idea that friends are forever; even politicians who need friends most do not hold that thought. It is a hypocritical philosophy. Life is measured by its performance, hence a friend without valuable contribution to you must be separated.

For a fact, everybody cannot be your friend. But then, you cannot build a bridge if you keep widening the river at the same time. Those who befriend everybody will have enough hands to pull them down. The reason is that, the best of friends are not many. Never many. If you have many people around you, be cautious of them, but enjoy their company. Know however that some of those who praise you do so because they are benefiting from you; those who curse you do so because they haven't gained from you. Praise singers are like pipers; you dictate their tunes by paying them.

There could be an executive meeting that is all about you, yet you are not invited. You will need someone to chip in a word for you someday, or else some resources you need to succeed as a manager will not be available. By that I mean some kind of a ways and means decisions when conclusions are drawn on who gets what, when, and how. Don't get me wrong, they want you to succeed, and will provide the resources to achieve it. Heaven helps you if someone is not out to outsmart, or get you fired. We call it management politics. That is when the organization makes decisions based on personality, rather than principle; and influence rather than necessity. It could also be rub-my-back-I-rub-yours kind of thing.

No manager has time for swings on the production floor. Associate and help as much as practicable, but keep your focus alive, right and directed. Depart from any friend who is not worth his/her salt; even Christ selected 12 out of many, 3 out of 12 and 1 out of 3. **Be pleasant to all, fair to many, good to some and special to few.** Those few matters a great deal. They matter to your matters. When you succeed, you will need them to keep your success afloat. Make your choice of friends without regrets. Be wise because **foolishness is an expensive venture**.

> Those who befriend everybody will have enough hands to pull him or her down. The reason is that best of friends are not many. Never many!

5.   **Save Time, Value Time, Invest Time**

In the human resources world, the least of staff is always accorded some entitlement in leave days each year. Most recognised of these are:

(i)   2 days of Sick Leave
(ii)   30mins of Short or Coffee Break
(iii)   60mins/1hr. Lunch Break
(iv)   14 days Annual Vacation/Leave
(v)   Saturday/Sunday – Weekend Off
(vi)   Public Holidays

With a total of 52 weeks, or 365 days or 8760 hours available for all forms of activities in a year, it behoves one to know that the largest proportion of our time is <u>NOT</u> actually invested in value-added activities or productive efforts.

The import here is the ironic truth that only few days are available for work. Incredible, you say, perhaps too incredible to admit. Well, managers do not have time for procrastinations. There is no productive time to waste. These facts are not disputable.

> Men have got to sit up, look up
> and face up and that very fast

67

It is a fact that a considerable amount of time is employed to yield little or nothing, summating at zero value, and destroying the fabrics of a great future.

Whoever values his time will not lose it. If you don't lose it, you will gain it, could you consider that one spend well over 200 days away from duty or work.

In the least extreme, a ridiculous balance yet exists where sick leave, vacation, public holidays and adjusted 16hrs off-duty are deducted from available days of the year.

Total no of days in the year: 365
        Less (provisions for)
                Sick leave   2
                Weekend offs (Sat/Sun)   104
                Public Holidays   5
                Off duty (16hrs daily)   160

                        Balance   94 days
                                          ===

Caution calls for Action! And Action calls for Caution!

68

Even where 94 days out of 365 days are available for work to reshape and direct an individual's life, it is few, though significant enough to make or mar a life and its succeeding generations. We need to realize that people have few days to colour their lives. Where wasted, it cannot be redeemed again. Wasted years must be consciously avoided. Time wasted runs into wasted hours, and wasted hours run into wasted days; wasted days run into wasted years and wasted years into wasted life. Caution, wisdom, duty and vision are the rules of a manager's game.

Suffice it to be reminded that time is not unlimited. You must thus value it enough to invest it productively. To secure optimum yield of investments, time must be well articulately utilized.

Forgive me to observe that there is no employer who planned well enough for their staff to be as rich as they were. Even the best of employees are paid, or offered, huge pay packets to enslave them. One notion could yet stem from the above analysis: the fact that every employee had opportunity to dictate his/her future since such a person had hundreds of days left to fashion his or her own future. No one had an excuse not to succeed.

6.   Procrastination: It's the manager's trap

Whatever can be done today, why fix for tomorrow?   The fact that there are intervening elements, which nullifies some scheduled agenda, does not make fool all other agenda.   Plans, purposes, agenda, and schedules must be drawn. Instead of baseless conclusions and sentiments, plans should be followed and programmes executed until evident realities dictate otherwise.

This is crucial because procrastination is a theft of time and a very subtle evil, which like a deadly virus, destroys the fabrics of a system without apology.

> **Men who procrastinate can't go far**

Procrastination slows down the pace of progress until it deadens it and grinds an organization to a fatal halt.   Imagine if every manager in the organization procrastinates. That company is destined for bankruptcy, if it's lucky. There is no absolute certainty that the change effected is the best for the programme or plan. Procrastination can be considered an aimless deferment of a reasonable action.   It often arose

70

out of a traveller's lack, a baseless fear, and a corruptive laziness. It ends in irreparable losses of efforts and resources. Managers must deal with the subtle evil of procrastination; otherwise, we would continue to pay for it.

Sometimes, indecision contributes to procrastination. Bad initial plans, shaky discourse, poor foresight, lack of determination, a nonchalant attitude and overbearing idleness; all play significant roles in procrastination. This explains why one who procrastinates often is always weak minded both to him and to the cause of others.

Chapter 4

BOARDROOM POLITICS

I cannot but address the politics that goes on in the boardroom. This is because this book is about reality of management. Every Manager has to understand that the boardroom had been deified more than it should. In several cases, the board room could be regarded as one or more of the following:

Jury Room
The Chairman Room
The best argument prevailing Room
The Board Secretary's' or Exec Dir's Room
The Confluence Room
The Financial Director's Room
The Rubber-stamp Room
The Nerd's Room

If you ever have a proposal for the approval of the board, you have to be ready and adequately prepared for it. I have seen Managers come to the board meetings on a premonition that their request will be an easy ride for approval; especially where the issue is contingent upon generic need that could likely be denied, e.g.

salaries and wages, benefits, office maintenance, production resources, upcoming conference, etc.

The fact is that good managers speak volumes at every opportunity they have to address the board, and they rarely know it. You must be good to marshal your point to the littlest possible argument in defence of your proposal.

Board Members Are Psychos: Yes we are. I was there. We begin to judge presentations first by who is talking

What is the issue?

Financial Costs involved

Significance to the organization

Time lag: Can we defer it or avoid it?

The irony is that we hold an impression of managers and their department by their presentations. Board members also judge future presentations by current presentations. In fact, when a manager was to be fired, the opinion of either a manager is a sluggard, inept, or capable individual is formed from their contact with the board. Same goes for promotion.

Be that as it may, your presentations to the board must be concise, adequate information (not necessarily sufficient) and convincing. You must defend your cause. Remember, there is a nerd in the room who will shred you apart, until you could prove your point. Most board members always follow the lead argument coming from one or two directors.

If you really want to do a unique thing for your department that need not die in its cradle, then play some politics prior to presenting it to the full board of directors. That is reach out to the most convincing directors, or some whose votes do swing others and let them know what you intend to do, and 'great' it is. It's called 'carrying them along'. If you are lackadaisical about it, it could end your career and future opportunities.

The benchmark is be good at what you do best.

Chapter 5
PRINCIPLE

What are principles? Take it that they are what differentiate principals from other people. This is my practical opinion of it. Principals are chiefs of opinions and pursuits. You can only keep principles (i.e. be a principal) at best if you are wealthy. Your true personality is better known when you are wealthy rather than when you are poor. If you are godly, humble, passionate, and resilient as a wealthy man, those are your true convictions. Poverty changes people like the colors of a chameleon. A poor man dumps standards and etiquette in the face of superior offers. Check out the differences between the convictions of a man in his poor state and in his wealthy state. How many rich men have kept the principles once held when they were poor?

> **When you are no longer poor, you will be a different man with different tastes**

Act like a Manager

There are lines of actions and operations that a man must responsibly take. Neither God nor man will do your duty for you; you have to do it. Managers who are religious need not use it as an excuse for laxity. Managers are called to act.

The scriptures state that 'God can do all things...' It never said, God will do all things. If you run your life on 'God will do all things for me', and resign yourself to impoverishing idleness and corruptive laziness then, you shall have what the Scriptures called 'poverty enough', 'poverty of a traveller and want like an armed man' (Prov.24: 33-34). Actually, faith should not be used as an excuse for slackness. Faith is action that is predicated on the word of God. Abraham believed and he departed, Isaac believed and he sowed, the widow of Zarephath believed and released her loaves of bread, Peter believed and walked on the water, the blind man believed and went to wash, the leper believed and was cleansed as he moved to wash. Name it, all those who believed also acted. They didn't believe and went to bed. You need to act, and take some form of action. This is applicable to all religions I know.

Someone once observed that poor people trust God more than the rich. Often, this may

76

not be correct because the poor always believe that God will do everything for them. To hold this notion is to be far from the truth and reality. No deception could be stronger!

> **You must act now!**

3-Fold Action Plan

Take specific course of action towards the realization of your age-long dreams. Christ taught us to get result by three-fold plan of action: Ask, Seek and Knock.

Where you must ask questions -- ask for help or favor, ask for direction-- do not hesitate to do so. Where you must seek for information to brighten your focus, directions and ultimate decisions, never hesitate. Several good things are available, but they must be sought out. In fact, the most valuable of world treasures– crude oil, gold, diamond, and crystal stones etc. --are hidden. They must be dug out. The most expensive beasts are in the thickest of forests. Cockroaches are less expensive than crickets; if you want them, you must find them out. Millions of dollars are being invested in discoveries, excavations and researches to find out great resources. Seeking is definitely strenuous and laborious, but it's with a target that's worth the toil. It may seem costly, but there is an invaluable benefit that could be derived from it. Just like a woman in travails, who will soon forget the regrettable pains of pushing to delivery, the pains of searching will be lost in the past when you get what you are looking for.

Where you have to knock, go ahead and do so. Never fear that you could be rejected or treated disdainfully. You may never predict the response to your request, so just go ahead and make the request. If nice, and pleasant fine; if not, thank God, turn your back, and fast-forward elsewhere. The fact that a door was closed against you does not dictate that all other doors will be. There is an abundance of hope for a man yet alive. Get on your feet and act. Get on your feet and lead your way out of doldrums.

> **Giant strides are not made while sitting; they are made while walking and working.**
> **Star players don't wait for the ball; they run in its direction**

3.   **Inspiration from a Star**
Managerial appointments are not often made by accidents. The fact that you got the job speaks volume. You are a unique personality and a shining star. That distinguishing personality had been recognized.

There is so much wisdom to draw from a star. In my study, I have learnt that over 40 sextillion Stars exist in our universe (Dakes, p1061), the Sun and Moon inclusive. In fact, the Sun, considered a dwarf star, is more than a million times bigger than the earth!

It is significant to learn that although the Sun is 93million miles away from the earth, we could feel its impact and yell at its scorching rays after noon.   The fiery impact of the Sun (remember, it's a dwarf star), I believe, is more than 2million bakeries put together. Such tremendous heat could melt a lot of stuff. It is also wonderful to know that some eyes could count about 3000 stars at nights. It is worthwhile to note that while some stars are fixed, others are interestingly magnetic, some are hidden or undiscovered and some of them could actually fall.

Permit that I submit that nature is a vivid, loud voice of the Supernatural, if only men could discern them. In the first instance, the immeasurable numbers of stars that flood the clouds convey the noble fact that each one of us can actually shine. You can shine. I can shine. Everyone could shine. I learnt this truth in my childhood from my mother. She taught us to believe that everyone could make a success and excel in their respective spheres. The sky is wide enough for all birds to fly without bumping into each other. Competition propels success and challenges everyone. It does not annihilate. Your success cannot disturb mine; neither can someone's progress block your chances. It's a pretty lie of the devil to think and draw erroneous conclusions that someone else's success would disturb us. No one has the capacity to overshadow you. No one! You are originally unique. Even scientifically, your thumbprint cannot be duplicated.

All stars shine

Secondly, no star seeks to be like the other; each maintains its distinctiveness and peculiarity. Imitations are proofs of limitation. They are evidences of failing capacity, which at their best, produces second best. Be original; it's the edge a genius has over his/her contemporaries anywhere in the world. Originality and ingenuity will forever be the hallmarks of distinctions.

Thirdly, a star cannot be covered. Thus, the belief that someone could cover the glory of another is an ancient myth invoked by the sorcerers and lazy folks. If nothing can cover the glory of the sun, no one can cover your glory. You are the only obstacle that could impede yourself. You will get to where you are going!

Fourthly, a star is big, many times the size of the earth; hence, you cannot choose to be small. Consider yourself as a big fellow treading the earth. The seed of the righteous shall be great upon the earth. Statistics have shown, for example, that children of the college educated parents are more likely to be college educated than others. Greatness only produces greatness. A great seed begets a great tree.

Fifthly, the fire of a star can devour beyond recovery. A star contains far more than the furnace of millions of bakeries. The spiritual implication is that you carry a spiritual firepower that could devour and destroy all hindrances utterly, with such holy potency that is stronger than that of an intercontinental ballistic missile.

Your holy fury is an unquenchable fire that all hell does dread.

Sixthly, stars are visible. Some eyes could count up to 3000 as informed. It is therefore untenable to complain that people discuss or talk about you. If you are nobody, you will not be a subject of discussion anywhere. If you are a success, a go-getter, an achiever, many people will definitely discuss you. For example, when the sun shines, people talk, if it does not, people talk. You need not waste your time over what people say about you because like Eleanor Roosevelt once noted:

"Great minds discuss ideas;
Average minds discuss events;
Small minds discuss people"

People discuss stars. They will talk about you. If not, you aren't there yet

---

In fact, you need to be bothered if people are not talking about you. It shows that you are not making progress enough for them to see. As soon as you hit a breakthrough or achieve a feat, people will talk about you. Celebrities make money by letting people talk about them.

It pays to be noticed as a News Maker not a News Reporter. Some people have a running career in News reporting yet they are not Journalists. They are successful gossipers and prominent rumour mongers, grapevine leaders, distinguished in the art of shameless reporting of unsubstantiated stories about people rather than issues. These "reporters" could be friends and colleagues who know a lot about you. They know every inch of your strides and thus report it with distortions. They broadcast it loud to quarters you haven't treaded. They have different reasons for their action. I will suggest you do 3 things about them:

❖ Make the news for them
❖ Walk tall to them
❖ Ignore their tales

They'll soon be tired or change batons as you keep making the news. You make the News and allow others tell the News!

Seventhly, stars are magnetic. If you consider yourself a star, you must be contagious. No one survives as a lone ranger. You must affect and be affected by others. Life is a two-way traffic, giving and taking. You must never die unfulfilled. Be fully fulfilled. Even in the search for prosperity, seek posterity. The future is superior to today. Yesterday is gone, not available to you; today is here at the junction of your best ability, but tomorrow is a mile away. Gather all your strengths together in readiness for it.

> Yesterday is opportunity gone, Today is opportunity here, and Tomorrow is opportunity on its way

Employ the best of wisdom to win all your adversaries. If there was an Ahitophel, enlist a Hushai, if they have seen your stars, relocate your base; if their Athalia shouted the 'treason', employ the 'reason'. Success is what opportunity makes ready, not accidents. Don't wait to jam luck, plan for it; walk towards it and work it through. You need not be measured by the longevity of your life but by its productivity; not by its duration but by its donation. The age of Methuselah has nothing to do with the wisdom of Solomon.

> Make Impact!

4. **Take Responsibility**

As a manager, the buck stops with you. You cannot blame your employee for the failures of your department. No executive wants to hear that. But how people behave at work is a function of what is going on in their lives.

There is an established fact that people act out of a 'remote cause of reaction'. This refers to a situation whereby you acted out of the normal state having been provoked by an instance not related to the current issue. For clarity, consider an instance whereby you extended your anger of disaffection to your official staff, because your nagging wife infuriated you from home.

There are people who fail in proper conduct and language when they are in need; when they are denied a privilege; when they are sick; when they recount some losses, etc. They will thus invoke their anger on anyone or anything that comes across them. If the goal for the day had to be achieved in your unit, you have to deal with the situation as at when it happens.

If you, as the manager, was having issues, you have to drop it at the entrance door right before your work starts. Your employee having a bad day, on the other hand, could be identified and the issues dealt with accordingly.

Actually, at some intense situations of life, people could be mad at everybody and everything around them. It would be amazing that some angers or reactions though justified, were offshoot of a remote cause(s) not related to the issue at hand.

These intense feelings and reactions could make you dislike not only people, but also systems around you. It is human to shift responsibility of one to another; if situations were normal, those abnormal reactions won't exist!

> It is natural to shift responsibility; it is supernatural to take responsibility

The bitter truth is that no one is responsible for another; everyone is responsible for himself/herself. There is no one saddled with the duty of leading you to where you wish to reach. Don't hold anyone guilty for yourself. You are responsible for yourself. Check out the palms of your hands, the lines on them are exclusively yours and permanently yours. They are neither exportable nor trade-able. They are yours. Hence, you are absolutely responsible for yourself. You have a similar instance in the biblical story of Naomi, the mother-in-law of Ruth. Naomi, whose name meant 'Pleasant', had rough experiences and incalculable bitterness due to the loss of her sons. She refused her good name and opted for the direct opposite i.e. 'Mara', which meant bitterness. She was mad at God. She was mad at men. She considered both God and men responsible for her misfortunes, and judged them guilty declaring 'the Almighty hath afflicted me' (Ruth 1:20-21). As a manager, consider that if things were well, you will ignore the faults of people. Do not blame anyone directly or indirectly for your misfortunes; take up your life as your responsibility. Look up to life as 'I am responsible for myself' rather than 'you are responsible for me'. Only God is absolutely dependable. As for men, they rarely sow where they don't expect to reap. They give to those who could return their favours, and share with those from whom they gain. This is the natural order and you belabour yourself changing it.

Be perfectly clear that, any help received from another was not a duty, but a privilege. Everyone is responsible for his own successes and failures. Those you may be looking up to for help, also worked their way up to their present status. Look for help from <u>above</u> not <u>abroad</u>, and claim with David that, *I will lift up my eyes unto the hills, from whence cometh my help, my help cometh from the Lord which made the Heaven and Earth* (Ps. 121:1-2).

When you take responsibility for yourself, you will be focused, directed and inspired to look up to God, pray hard, work hard and be free of heart-aches caused by trust in mortal, frail humans. It seems to me that men and women expect too much from themselves.

Ask – How do I solve this.......?

Not – Who will solve this for me?

God can raise helpers for you as He did for David

5. **Managerial Honour**

The reposition of honour demands

(a)   a honourable personality

(b)   a honourable performance.

It may not be enough to hold a distinguished personality; a distinguished performance need also be its complement. In the purview of personality, such coordinated areas of character traits and tutored temperaments, are required.

To be effective, managers must not only have education, good appearance, knowledge, experience, and ability to do the job. They must also have the initiative, perseverance, stability, leadership, self-reliance, and a sense of loyalty that the position requires.

Consequently, the honour of a man is not only reposed in his education, experience, knowledge, among others; it is also in his industry, stability, perseverance, and association. In fact, the combination of these factors makes the whole person, and is directly impacted on performance.

An honourable performance is a product of personality and parameters examined earlier on.

Chapter 5

PROSPERITY

Negotiate: A Better Deal
The everyday life of a manager is about deals, and negotiations. You consult with executives to have the best materials and people to accomplish tasks, and negotiate with employees to complete tasks assigned.

Life too, is a choice. Living, walking, crawling or running. They are choices made principally by men and women. The sphere of operations has enough rooms created for everyone to be as tall or high as one could ever wish.

Check this out! The cloud above the head of over 6 billion people on the earth is wide enough to contain them, without any head-on-collision in space. No head disturbs the other from occupying its own space. An adage says, the cloud is wide enough for all birds to fly without bumping one another. For sure however, fingers are not equal, thus estates of men are determined by several parameters, which set men either at high or low places, either as rulers, or as the ruled; either as masters or as servants.

The mystery of life is that it creates positions for both the high and the low; the rich and poor; the leaders and the led; the kings and the subject; but perhaps does not decree who should occupy them. God wishes all men well. It is men who choose their path and thus their positions. Do not be caught in the web of debate on inconclusive issues like destiny, but pursue destinations! If you succeed, men say it is your destiny because you have reached a point of your destination. We all face our destinations, which others call destiny.

> **Don't ache your head about destiny, pursue your destinations**

No one is created outside the "fearfully and wonderfully made" notion (Ps. 139:14); hence no one is actually an outcast in God's eye. The choice of men, leads them to their destinations. When a man has run his life in full cycle, others then christened what he has made up, as destiny. One could then note that whatever men called 'destiny', actually submits to destinations. Reach your destination, and leave other men to define destiny for you.

There is a world of difference between News Makers and News Reporters. Everyone makes the choice of where he treads. Be a News Maker and leave News Reporters to report your exploits and successes.

> **You Make the News**
> **Others Break the News!**

The essence of the foregoing is to see you negotiate for a better deal as you make choices that single you out to limelight. Tell life where you are going, and run after it!

In negotiation, the bargaining power of the parties could determine how much they get. If your bargaining power is strong enough to secure what you deserved, you'll get it. This explains why I had always posited that you could get what you deserve if you negotiate well for it. In the Moses-Pharaoh negotiation, Moses was strong. While Pharaoh offered limited liberty (via permission to go but not very far), Moses negotiated for and got perfect freedom, unconditional liberty. Sincerely, the storms of life could toughen your skin to provide you with a strong bargaining power for all that life offers. Don't be afraid of growing tough skin. The wisdom reads, 'He trains my hands to war, so that a bow of steel is broken by it' (Ps 18:34).At best, circumstances only strengthen, they won't sink you.

> **If you know what you're looking for, negotiate for it!**

Those whose names have been listed as world geniuses, inventors and great men have either had no predecessor or had predecessors whose works didn't result into theirs. They were not discouraged for those reasons. Your success is not dependent on whether someone else ever succeeded in like manner or not. **Heroism is available for all to achieve.** Everyone is allowed to bid for it with sufficient rooms for all bidders to win. **There is no loser-bidder but only those who are yet to win!**

> **Negotiate for Peaks!**

2.   Service is Superior to Money
The writer of Eccl. 10:19 taught that *"money answereth all things"*. This needs be understood from its proper context. The fact that money

93

answers all things, does not confirm that the answer will always be correct. Even the author-King Solomon had cases that money could not have answered correctly. He prayed for wisdom rather than riches, God's people rather than himself.

Certainly, money does pose answers to all things. Several people believe that they can get anything done if there was sufficient money to match the request, either by outright purchase or payment for needed service. The entire system of operations in the world is monetised. People and Nations are graded by the amount of money they possess. The old time trade was carried out via exchange of acceptable means of currency. Hence, there is no doubt that money had for a long time, been instrument of transactions among nations and people. Various levels of riches and possessions stratify societies. Yet, money is not, and can never be, everything. Never!

Simply stated, money answers all things, but all its answers cannot always be correct. A student may answer the required number of questions before the expiration of the examination time. He might have answered them as per instructions and guidelines, yet may not score 100%. Money may answer all things, but some of its answers may not be correct. Even King Solomon, knows.

Today, money is an idol, riches are gods and prosperity is the most fascinating subject. The full dimension of an intrinsic desire to prosper and be rich, should include the ultimate desire to serve and provide service. After all, Lazarus <u>died</u> and he was buried; the rich man also <u>died</u> and he was buried. The only legacy that a true giant could leave behind is the number of lives he had positively affected. While we seek avenues to improve on our lives and be wealthy, we must bear the concern to lend a serving hand to those in need.

Indeed, the rich are in a vantage position to serve better and engage in philanthropic endeavours, community service, educational supports and human services. The acquisition of wealth is useless without distribution of service to the needy, the orphans, the widows and the physically challenged. The unique line of difference between the rich and the poor is the grace of God, which didn't permit his investment risks to drown him. An adage says that if the hunter recall the pains, anguish and sufferings in the forest, he will not share his booties. When

consideration is given to lines of expenditure, paramount items should include:
- ➤ Operational expenses
- ➤ Salaries & emoluments
- ➤ Projects/Developmental efforts
- ➤ Benevolence

Having been engaged in services to young people for well over 10 years, I can confidently assure that human services are a unique and rewarding experience. Uplifting the falling, providing strength to the weak, assuring the helpless, feeding the hungry, educating a nation, sharing some love, propagating peace, supporting the community are genuine and noble fields in which to invest.

3.   Posterity is Superior to Prosperity
Greatness is best evaluated by a man's contribution to his world. Landslides best define legacies. Legacies are best defined by their impact on men. It is indeed cheery news that the life of an individual has impacted positively on that of another, alleviating pains and banishing sorrows. Life at best, is best, when it had been invested in making another life its best.

> **Landslides best define legacies. Legacies are best defined by their impact on men**

I will enjoin anyone who ever had a contact with this piece to pursue greatness, wealth and peaks in life, with the prime purpose of investing them in service to humanity. Prosperity is indeed useless without posterity. Let me point accurately that footprints of men are evident in three ways. People will remember you for what you were. You can choose which footprint you intend to leave.

1st Instance:*Those you have met or related with, wished at your departure, that you never passed their way again. They have had a previous dosage of all that you ever had to offer. In their minds, you are unwanted, detested and rejected. They wished that someone like you would never cross them again. You could thus be a sad story to them.*

2nd Instance:*Those you had met or related with, took no cognisance of your presence or absence. In their minds, they are in no-way aware of your impact, either to them, or others around them. You existed as if you never really did. It's a tasteless situation to be in, and such is an unrewarding life. To them, you never touched any life with your presence.*

3rd Instance. *Those you had met or related with, never wished you depart from them. In their minds, they hold a passionate desire to see you, or someone like you passing their way again, and*

97

again. Your relationship with them was that of a unique-love-help-service affair. Your footprint to them was golden, and your remembrance desirably pleasant. If privileged, they will wish to have you again.

Above shows three types of men, which describe all of us. We must endeavour to be listed in the 3rdcategory. Kindness is not expensive. What you cannot offer in cash, you can offer in kind. What you cannot offer in efforts, you can offer in sweet objective counsels. If you don't have a gift to offer, please give a smile, throw a hug, give a kiss and offer a handshake. If you can't solve a man's problem, don't dear add to it!

Posterity is superior to prosperity. What you are to other men, is greater than what you have acquired. The heart is bigger than the head, any day.

Make History, Make it Today!

The Making of a Giant

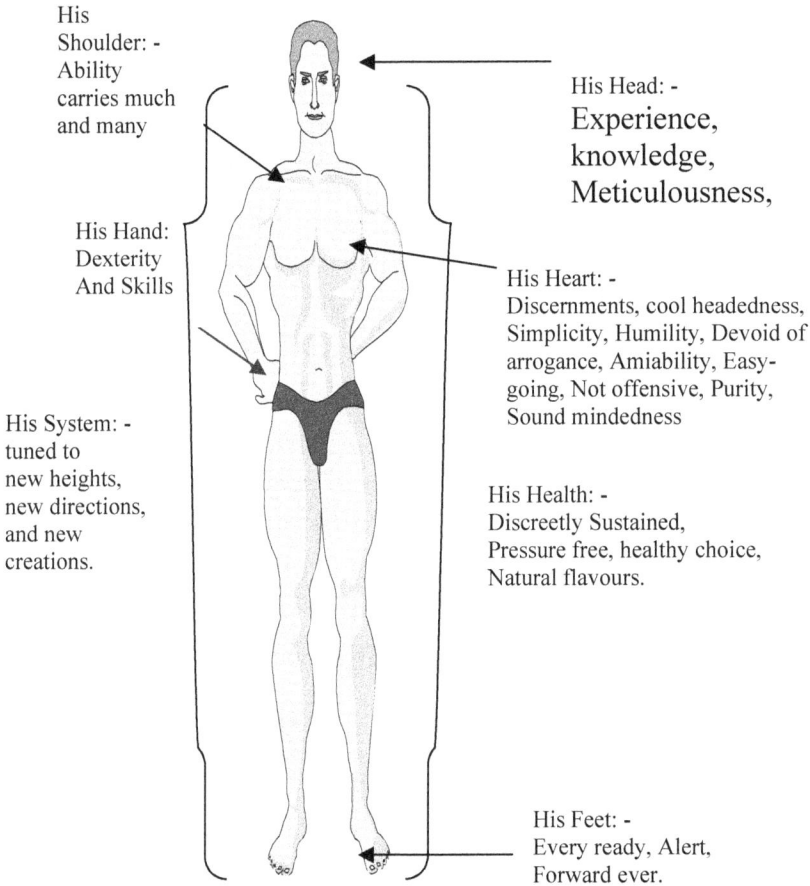

His Shoulder: - Ability carries much and many

His Hand: Dexterity And Skills

His System: - tuned to new heights, new directions, and new creations.

His Head: - Experience, knowledge, Meticulousness,

His Heart: - Discernments, cool headedness, Simplicity, Humility, Devoid of arrogance, Amiability, Easy-going, Not offensive, Purity, Sound mindedness

His Health: - Discreetly Sustained, Pressure free, healthy choice, Natural flavours.

His Feet: - Every ready, Alert, Forward ever.

The above diagram vividly conveys an artistic impression of giant star personality and all his make-up. It is a simple analogy of the ideas shared in this book for anyone who wishes to be great and achieve stardom.

CONCLUSION

The conclusion of the whole matter is for you to decide to make it big and succeed excellently. **Let it be a choice to be a successful manager in any field you find yourself.**
To be a Winner;
To be a Success and;
To be Great.
No matter the obstacles, no matter the backgrounds, no matter the challenges, no matter the odds against the upward surge, **Remember that the star will always shine, no matter how dark the night may turn. No one can hold the appearance of the Sun. No matter how long the night becomes, the day will yet appear.** You are on your way up!
I'll see you at the top!

…intentionally left blank….

Synopsis

The book is meant to reach one manager
who at the moment is not 'rich' nor own
huge sources of wealth but could transform
himself or herself into a formidable
personality and a great icon.

Bibliography

Machiavelli, Niccolo. *The Prince,* translated by N.H. Thomson. Vol. XXXVI, Part 1. The Harvard Classics. New York: P.F. Collier & Son, 1909–14; Bartleby.com

Dakes Annotated Concordance Bible (2012). Dake Publishing Inc., Lawrenceville, GA.

Umesh Ramakrishnan (2008). There's no Elevator to the Top. Penguin Books, New York.

Zig Ziglar (2003).*Top Performance.* Fleming H. Revell, Michigan.

www.ingramcontent.com/pod-product-compliance
Lightning Source LLC
Chambersburg PA
CBHW060630210326
41520CB00010B/1547